A Beginning-to-Read Book

Being Kind to Our Planet

by Mary Lindeen

NORWOOD HOUSE PRESS

DEAR CAREGIVER, The *Beginning to Read—Read and Discover* books provide emergent readers the opportunity to explore the world through nonfiction while building early reading skills. The text integrates both common sight words and content vocabulary. These key words are featured on lists provided at the back of the book to help your child expand his or her sight word recognition, which helps build reading fluency. The content words expand vocabulary and support comprehension.

Nonfiction text is any text that is factual. The Common Core State Standards call for an increase in the amount of informational text reading among students. The Standards aim to promote college and career readiness among students. Preparation for college and career endeavors requires proficiency in reading complex informational texts in a variety of content areas. You can help your child build a foundation by introducing nonfiction early. To further support the CCSS, you will find Reading Reinforcement activities at the back of the book that are aligned to these Standards.

Above all, the most important part of the reading experience is to have fun and enjoy it!
Sincerely,

Shannon Cannon

Shannon Cannon, Ph.D.
Literacy Consultant

Norwood House Press

For more information about Norwood House Press please visit our website at www.norwoodhousepress.com or call 866-565-2900.
© 2021 Norwood House Press. Beginning-to-Read™ is a trademark of Norwood House Press.

Editor: Judy Kentor Schmauss
Designer: Sara Radka

Photo Credits:
Getty Images, cover, 4-29; Pixabay, 3; Shutterstock, 1

Library of Congress Cataloging-in-Publication Data
Title: Being kind to our planet / by Mary Lindeen.
Description: Chicago : Norwood House Press, [2021] | Series: A beginning-to-read book | Audience:
    Grades K-1 | Summary: "All people need a healthy planet to live on, so choosing to be kind to Earth
    by caring for its air, land, and water benefits everyone. An early social-emotional learning book that
    includes a note to caregivers, reading activities, and a word list"— Provided by publisher.
Identifiers: LCCN 2019048915 (print) | LCCN 2019048916 (ebook) | ISBN 9781684508945 (hardcover) |
    ISBN 9781684045167 (paperback) | ISBN 9781684045204 (epub)
Subjects: LCSH: Environmental education—Juvenile literature.
Classification: LCC GE115 .L56 2020 (print) | LCC GE115 (ebook) | DDC 333.7071—dc23
LC record available at https://lccn.loc.gov/2019048915
LC ebook record available at https://lccn.loc.gov/2019048916

Hardcover ISBN: 978-1-68450-894-5
Paperback ISBN: 978-1-68404-516-7

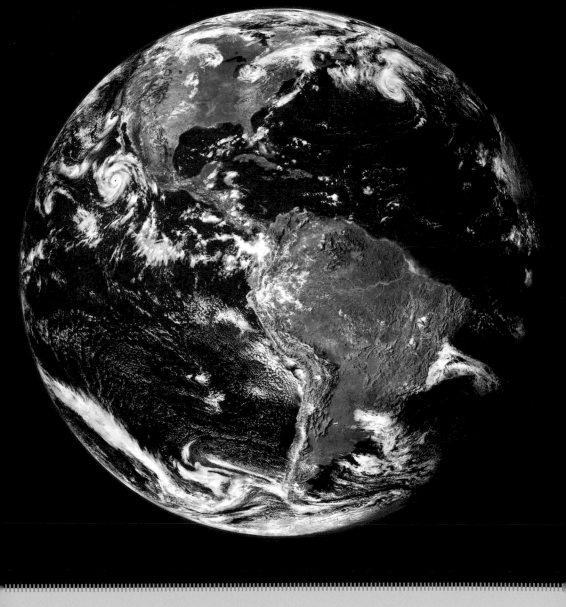

This is our planet.

Our planet gives us air to breathe.

It gives us water to drink.

It gives us land to live and play on.

Our planet helps
us stay strong
and healthy.

We can help our
planet stay strong
and healthy, too.

We can be kind
to it.

We can take care
of our air.

We can walk
or bike.

That helps keep
our air clean.

We can use
less energy.

That helps keep
our air clean, too.

Turning off lights
we don't need
saves energy.

We can take care
of our water.

We can turn off
faucets when we're
not using them.

That saves water.

Taking shorter
baths and showers
saves water, too.

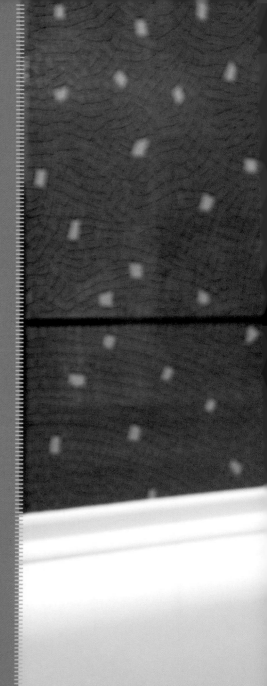

We can put garbage where it belongs.

That keeps litter out of rivers, lakes, and oceans.

We can take care
of our land.

We can plant
trees and flowers.

We can make
our land beautiful.

What is **not** beautiful?
Trash!

We can make less trash by
reusing and recycling things.

We can also
clean up our land.

We can clean up
our school grounds
and parks.

Everyone can be kind to our planet.

We can all help care for its air, water, and land.

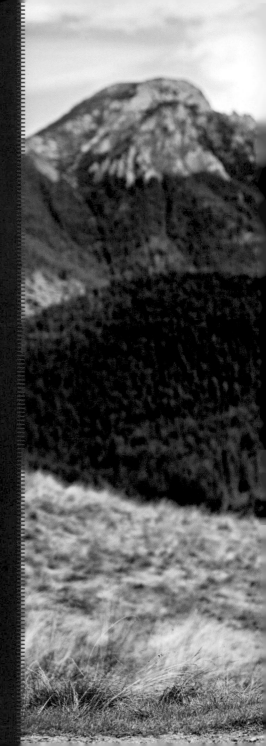

That makes our
planet safer
and healthier
for all of us!

. . . READING REINFORCEMENT. . .

CRAFT AND STRUCTURE

To check your child's understanding of the organization of the book, recreate the following chart on a sheet of paper. Read the book with your child, and then help him or her fill in the chart using what they learned. Work together to complete the chart by writing words or ideas from the book that tell about ways to be kind to our planet.

air	
water	
land	

VOCABULARY: Learning Content Words

Content words are words that are specific to a particular topic. All of the content words in this book can be found on page 32. Use some or all of these content words to complete one or more of the following activities:

• Have your child name the synonym/antonym of the word.

• Ask your child to find word parts/smaller words within a word.

• Write the words' definitions on cards; mix up the cards and have your child choose the correct definition.

• Help your child find the commonalities between words.

• Sort the words into different groups; for example, by number of letters, sounds, categories, etc.

FOUNDATIONAL SKILLS: Consonant Blends

Consonant blends are two consonants together that each make their own sound within a single syllable. Consonant blends are usually found at the beginning or end of a word. Have your child identify the consonant blends in the list of words below. Then help your child find words with consonant blends in this book.

broke	grass	flute
point	friendly	sand

CLOSE READING OF INFORMATIONAL TEXT

Close reading helps children comprehend text. It includes reading a text, discussing it with others, and answering questions about it. Use these questions to discuss this book with your child:

- How does taking a shorter shower save water?
- What is an example of something you might reuse?
- What is an example of something you might recycle?
- How does having clean water affect our health?
- Why does riding a bike help save the air?
- What is something you do that is kind to our planet?

FLUENCY

Fluency is the ability to read accurately with speed and expression. Help your child practice fluency by using one or more of the following activities:

- Reread the book to your child at least two times while he or she uses a finger to track each word as it is read.
- Read a line of the book, then reread it as your child reads along with you.
- Ask your child to go back through the book and read the words he or she knows.
- Have your child practice reading the book several times to improve accuracy, rate, and expression.

··· Word List ···

Being Kind to Our Planet uses the 83 words listed below. *High-frequency words* are those words that are used most often in the English language. They are sometimes referred to as *sight words* because children need to learn to recognize them automatically when they read. *Content words* are any words specific to a particular topic. Regular practice reading these words will enhance your child's ability to read with greater fluency and comprehension.

High-Frequency Words

air	give(s)	off	take(ing)	us
all	help(s)	on	that	use(ing)
also	is	or	them	water
and	it	our	things	we
be	its	out	this	what
by	make(s)	play	to	when
can	not	put	too	where
for	of	school	up	

Content Words

baths	energy	kind	parks	showers
beautiful	everyone	lakes	planet	stay
belongs	faucets	land	plant	strong
bike	flowers	less	recycling	trash
breathe	garbage	lights	reusing	trees
care	grounds	litter	rivers	turn(ing)
clean	health(ier)	live	safer	walk
don't	healthy	need	saves	we're
drink	keep(s)	oceans	shorter	

··· About the Author

Mary Lindeen is a writer, editor, parent, and former elementary school teacher. She has written more than 100 books for children and edited many more. She specializes in early literacy instruction and books for young readers, especially nonfiction.